Table of Contents

Chapter 1 – Introduction

When the Soviet Union collapsed under its own financial strain in 1991, it would have been foolish to forecast a similar fate for the United States. Twenty years later, budget deficits and national debt are major liabilities to American sovereignty. America's expenditures on three operations since 11 September 2001-Operation Noble Eagle, Operation Enduring Freedom, and Operation Iraqi Freedom- totaled $1.283 trillion as of May 2011.[1] These expenditures, and the American defense budget in general, have come under the crosshairs of public discourse. Today, political leaders, military leaders, and the American public agree that such spending is unsustainable over the long run.

The Department of Defense's (DoD) appreciation for the gravity of the American economic situation is evident across the board. Chairman of the Joint Chiefs of Staff, Admiral Mike Mullen repeatedly identified national debt as America's greatest security risk in speeches and press releases since June 2010. Defense Secretary Robert Gates said "My hope and expectation is that as a result of these changes over time, what had been a culture of endless money, where cost was rarely a consideration, will become a culture of savings and restraint" when he announced $78 billion in DoD budget cuts in January 2011.[2] Undersecretary of Defense for Acquisition, Technology, and Logistics, Ashton Carter reinforced Gates' sentiment when he said the DoD needs "better value for the defense dollar."[3] After nearly a decade of free spending,

---

[1] Amy Belasco, *The Cost of Afghanistan, Iraq, and Other Global War on Terror Operations Since 9/11* (Washington, DC: Congressional Research Service, 2011), 1.

[2] Charley Keyes, "Defense Secretary Announces Billions in Budget Cuts," *CNN.com*, 6 January 2011, http://articles.cnn.com/2011-01-06/politics/pentagon.budget.cuts_1_ defense-budget-gates-plan-defense-secretary-robert-gates?_s=PM:POLITICS (accessed 20 March 2011).

[3] Donna Miles, "Carter: Budget Cuts Demand More DoD Buying Power," *American Forces Press Service*, 20 April 2011, http://www.defense.gov/news/newsarticle.aspx?id= 63633 (accessed 20 March 2011).

American political and military leaders now regard defense costs with increased scrutiny, driving the Department of Defense toward greater efficiency.

This monograph examines airpower and heavy ground combat power to consider whether one of these force components is more effective and efficient than the other. To do so, it reviews each component's technological advances and theory development to show how each force is employed in the modern operational environment. The monograph includes a model to illustrate functions, missions, and tasks that each component performs. In comparison, the model shows how each force's fundamental characteristics either promote or inhibit efficiency for the roles it fulfills.

But what is efficiency, and can a military force be effective in operations while being efficient? Webster's defines "effective" as an adjective that means "adequate to accomplish a purpose; producing the intended or expected result."[4] In the plain English, military context, this means that our forces must be capable of achieving operational objectives that support an overall strategic end state. Webster's lists "efficient" as another adjective, meaning "performing or functioning in the best possible manner with the least waste of time and effort; having and using requisite knowledge, skill, and industry; competent; capable."[5] This definition of "efficient" seems to incorporate many of the qualities of "effective," but it places time and effort measurement criteria upon the merit of something's effectiveness, linking the two words together. Military professionals do not normally recognize this linkage.

Military professionals typically seek effectiveness while ignoring efficiency, for the two concepts are often thought to be mutually exclusive in decisive operations. Terms like "mass," "reserve," "reinforcement," and "redundancy" come to mind while planning to wield decisive

---

[4]Dictionary.com, s.v. "Effective," http://dictionary.reference.com/browse/effective (accessed 20 March 2011).

[5]Dictionary.com, s.v. "Efficient," http://dictionary.reference.com/browse/efficient (accessed 20 March 2011).

combat power against an adversary at the chosen time and place. Even Undersecretary Carter conceded that supporting troops in conflict is "an area where efficiency comes in, too, but effectiveness is most of the challenge."[6] Operational artists yearn to mass three, four, even six times the combat power of the adversary at a decisive point in order to achieve victory in offensive operations, even if that means that great portions of that combat power go unused in the decisive battle.

In the past, such overwhelming firepower on the battlefield was desirable, for in the end winning was what really mattered. Today, there are two major drawbacks to the mantra of overwhelming the enemy with combat power on the battlefield. First, as discussed in the opening paragraphs, it costs a lot more to assemble huge fielded forces in distant places. The accumulating costs of two major regional conflicts have weakened American power on the global stage over the last decade. Second, the lethality of modern weapons, as first seen during the Arab-Israeli conflict in 1973, means a lot more blood and treasure is lost on the modern battlefield. Slugfests between heavy forces in the modern operational environment exude far higher costs, in both money and lives, than they did in the past.

Heavy ground forces have typically been the hallmark of decisive combat power since the emergence of the tank during World War I. Historian Robert Citino writes that "Both world wars, the 'minor' but still sanguinary conflicts like Korea, the Iran-Iraq War, Operation Desert Storm, and just about every other occasion for hostilities since 1917 have featured armor in a prominent battlefield role."[7] Originally conceived as an indestructible tool to break through the fixed trenches of World War I's Western Front, tanks displayed their vulnerability on the battlefield time and again as countermeasures kept pace with armored offensive and defensive capabilities. Despite their liabilities, heavy forces retain favor with military professionals for the

---

[6]Miles, "Carter: Budget Cuts Demand More DoD Buying Power."

[7]Robert Citino, *Armored Forces: History and Sourcebook* (Westport, CT: Greenwood Press, 1994), 149.

tactical mobility and the firepower they bring to the battlefield, considered an essential part of maneuver warfare. This firepower and tactical mobility, however, brings with it the burden of massive operational logistics requirements and diminished operational reach.

Could airpower be the answer to the shortcomings in armored forces? Early airpower theorists such as William "Billy" Mitchell and Giulio Douhet certainly thought so. Mitchell wrote in *Winged Defense* that airpower produces "quick and lasting results that are less expensive than land armies and navies."[8] Both he and Douhet believed that airpower was virtually unstoppable in offensive operations. Both were proved wrong in World War II, when the Army Air Corps lost over 115,000 airmen, when to survive through thirty missions was considered a significant accomplishment.[9] Despite these earlier beliefs to the contrary, airpower also revealed offensive shortcomings during the Second World War, failing to achieve the decisive effects touted by the likes of Mitchell and Douhet. What is more, like heavy ground forces, airpower assets carry significant logistical requirements to the fight. The only difference is that airpower logistical constraints surface far behind the front lines.

This monograph sheds light on the topics of effectiveness and efficiency by comparing the capabilities, requirements, and vulnerabilities of air forces and heavy ground forces during major combat operations. The monograph uses an exploratory study to highlight areas of overlap between the two forces, and to identify areas where each force is unique. It outlines the historical development of each force since its inception in the early twentieth century, discusses the preeminent theories regarding employment of each force, and looks to American conflicts in the post-Cold War era to cite specific uses of each force. The study seeks to identify the American way of war that first developed in AirLand Battle of the 1980s and carried through to the modern era. It specifically shows how air forces and heavy ground forces have been used in recent

[8]William Mitchell, *Winged Defense* (New York: Putnam's Sons, 1927), 14.

[9]Department of the Army, "Army Battle Casualties and Non-Battle Deaths in World War II" (Report, Washington, DC, 25 June 1953), 6.

conflicts from Operation Desert Storm to Operation Odyssey Dawn. Finally, it compares the relative strengths and weaknesses of each fighting element to determine its relationship to effectiveness, efficiency, and overall contribution to operational art.

Chapters 2 and 3 outline the historical development of heavy ground power and airpower from each component's inauguration in World War I. The opening chapter examines technical capabilities that were conceived and built into each force component, and the countermeasures developed in response to those emergent capabilities. It also includes discussion and analysis of the most influential thinkers during the process of each force's development, including Douhet, Mitchell, Boyd, and Warden on the airpower side, and Fuller, Von Seeckt, Guderian, and De Gaulle on the heavy ground power side. Each chapter concludes with a summary of modern doctrine pertaining to each respective force component.

The fourth chapter compares heavy ground power to airpower through a model. The model, derived from contents of the previous two chapters, shows how each component's fundamental characteristics drive the way it is employed using operational art. It shows where each force component is unique and where the two components' capabilities overlap. From there, it illustrates the tasks and missions that each component performs based on its inherent capabilities. The model shows how tasks and missions vary for each fighting component based on their foundational characteristics.

Chapter 5 includes a very brief synopsis of the topics of effectiveness, efficiency, and efficacy. It looks to some of history's most prominent theorists to convey the importance of efficacy in fighting forces.

Chapter 6 includes case studies on Operation Desert Storm and Operation Iraqi Freedom. The case studies highlight specific evidence of each force's employment in those conflicts. It wraps up with a comparison of the two conflicts to draw conclusions about why coalition forces were victorious in major combat operations in both circumstances.

The final chapter reviews and summarizes the research and findings drawn from the monograph's earlier sections. It draws conclusions about the comparison of heavy ground power to airpower to determine what, if anything, should be done about future force composition and joint doctrine.

Chapter 2 – Armor Capabilities, Theory, and Doctrine

The horrors of trench warfare in World War I made deep impressions on military theorists around the world. Military leaders were deeply disturbed by the wasteful spillage of blood and treasure along the Western Front. In response, inventors and theorists sought technological solutions to tip the balance of forces along the trenches and gain a decisive advantage over the enemy. Their goal was to create a machine that would protect friendly forces while challenging the enemy with an asymmetric and indefensible threat. Two major technologies emerged from these efforts. Tanks were invented, designed, built, and employed during the course of the war. Aircraft, though existent before World War I, evolved from simple observation platforms into true aerial fighting machines.

This chapter briefly outlines capabilities of heavy ground forces and airpower from their beginnings through the modern era. It focuses on the capability requirements that the two force components were originally designed to fill, and the progression of additional capabilities discovered after each force component's introduction. The chapter also discusses weapons and countermeasures designed to diminish the effects of each component's capabilities. Finally, Chapter 1 reviews the most influential theories during each component's lifetime, arriving at modern doctrinal capabilities.

Heavy ground maneuver forces were born in the form of tanks on the Western Front in World War I. British Lieutenant Colonel E. D. Swinton conceived tanks as a means to break the stalemate along the trench lines between Germany and France. In 1914, Swinton visualized "a power-driven, bullet-proof armed engine, capable of destroying machine guns, of crossing country and trenches, of breaking through entanglements, and of climbing earthworks."[10] After two years of research and development, General Douglas Haig first employed tanks in battle on 15 September 1916, near the villages of Flers and Courcellette in France.[11] Haig used far fewer tanks than were called for by early British armored doctrine, and they had little impact on the battle. The first tanks subjected their crews to deplorable conditions, were barely capable of traveling at four miles per hour, were mechanically unreliable, and were rather vulnerable to machine gun fire due to shortcomings in their armor.

Despite their underwhelming debut, tanks gained favor with military practitioners during World War I. British engineers refined tank designs numerous times in a single year, and by autumn 1917 they produced the Mark IV model. Tanks finally made important contributions to victory on the battlefield when the British Mark IVs penetrated German lines at Cambrai on 20 November 1917.[12] Notably, famed armored warfare theorist Lieutenant Colonel J. F. C Fuller got his start at Cambrai as the British "Tank Corps" Chief of Staff. By the end of the war, armored forces were important, although not decisive to the overall Allied victory.

World War I gave rise to two main trends from the interwar period to the modern era – developments in technology and developments in armored warfare theory. The first section below reviews technological developments, the second section discusses theory, and the third section highlights modern Heavy Brigade Combat Team and Combined Arms Battalion doctrine.

Armor Technology

Armored technology has progressed markedly since the days of E. D. Swinton's first effort in 1914. Technological improvements in armored machines have been primarily for the

---

[10]Ernest .D. Swinton, *Eyewitness* (London: Hodder and Stoughton, 1932), 79.

[11]Citino, *Armored Forces; History and Sourcebook*, 13.

[12]Ibid., 18.

purposes of survivability and lethality. Although tanks enjoyed advances in both categories during their evolution, anti-tank countermeasures kept pace with virtually every tank improvement.

Swinton's first design called for a machine capable of four mile-per-hour speed in both forward and reverse, to make 90-degree turns at full speed, to cross earthen parapets up to five feet high, to cross gaps up to five feet wide, and to have a combat radius of 20 miles.[13] Furthermore, it was to carry ten men, be armed with two machine guns and one light gun, and have a maximum weight of 14 tons.[14] The resulting machine featured 10-millimeter frontal armor, 8-millimeter side armor, two 57-millimeter guns, and three machine guns.[15] Although the tank was relatively impervious to machine gun fire, its vision slits were still vulnerable to penetration, and it was certainly vulnerable to grenades and artillery. The only problems with field artillery were its incapacity to quickly shift fires against moving targets in close proximity and the exposure of artillerymen to machine gun fires from tanks and their supporting infantry.

While tanks in World War one were able to produce shallow penetrations at Cambrai in 1917, and later at Amiens, they never achieved a deep and lasting penetration as envisioned by J. F. C. Fuller in his "Plan 1919." Tank designers and anti-tank weapon designers went back to the drawing boards during the interwar period, focusing on better machines and better ways to kill them. World War II intensified efforts on both sides of the equation. Numerous improvements in armor, mobility and weaponry resulted from these efforts.

Tank joints transitioned from rivets to welds and shapes became more sloped to deflect incoming projectiles. Armor utilized many of the benefits discovered from naval armor. These measures served to overcome the ever-increasing size of projectiles designed to kill tanks. By

---

[13]Ibid., 10.

[14]Ibid., 11.

[15]Ian Hogg, *Tank Killing: Anti-Tank Warfare by Men and Machines* (New York: Sarpedon, 1996), 4.

1940, the face-hardened armor could shatter up to 75-millimeter projectiles on contact.[16] Tanks also saw improvements in firepower and mobility. Main guns got larger, up to 75 millimeters in the French Char B1, and British and German tank speeds exceeded 30 miles per hour.[17] By the end of World War II, tanks were faster, tougher, and far more lethal than their predecessors in the Great War.

Weapon designers made large strides to keep pace with tanks' ever-increasing lethality and protective improvements. During World War I and the early interwar period, gun makers only had to increase projectile calibers to match corresponding improvements in armor technology. Over time, however, two main limitations forced inventors to become more creative with their solutions. First, as projectile calibers became larger, gun mobility decreased, making gun crews highly vulnerable to tank and machine gun fire on the battlefield. The sheer size and weight of towed guns also made it nearly impossible to quickly reorient them to their fast-moving targets. The solution was to mount guns on tracked, motorized chassis much like their motor borne adversaries – enter a main component of modern armored warfare: self-propelled artillery.

The second problem facing weapon designers was the unwinnable tradeoff between projectile velocity and shot shatter. Specifically, as tank armor got thicker, higher projectile velocities were needed to penetrate that armor. Required projectile speed was so high that rounds would shatter, rather than penetrate armor. Capped shells were the first answer, but after they would not penetrate armor weapon designers eventually developed the Armor Piercing Discarding Sabot (APDS). APDS made it possible to shoot a comparatively heavy projectile at extremely high velocities. Released just before the Normandy invasion, APDS helped secure

---

[16]Ibid., 13.

[17]Citino, *Armored Forces; History and Sourcebook*, 59.

Allied victories over the Nazis in World War II, with its ability to penetrate 146 millimeters of armor at 1000 meters.[18]

After World War II, weapons designers unveiled several ways to kill tanks. First, the British developed the recoilless gun and high explosive shaped charge projectile to go with it. This system created a much more tactically mobile, yet equally lethal weapon to its traditional counterpart. Additionally, by the early 1950s, the French, British, Soviets, and Australians all had anti-tank guided missile (AGTM) development programs underway.[19] These steerable, high explosive projectiles were far more lethal than their predecessors.

By 1973, AGTMs and rocket-propelled grenades were important factors to the outcome of the Arab-Israeli conflict in the Middle East. Military professionals around the world watched closely in what became a surprisingly lethal combat environment. Leaders on both sides of the Cold War were alarmed about the tanks' vulnerability to modern weapon systems. They sought new means to enhance survivability on the battlefield, leading to the Israeli invention of explosive reactive armor (ERA), and increased emphasis on rotary and fixed-wing offensive systems by the superpowers. Most other nations incorporated ERA into their own systems shortly after the Israeli invention.

The Arab-Israeli war also spurred designers to develop an entirely new generation of tanks in the 1970s and 1980s, resulting in the American M-1, the British Challenger, and the West German Leopard 2, with corresponding T-series tanks on the Soviet side. The new generation of tanks was considerably more mobile, lethal, and defensible than the previous generation. For example, the M-1's turbine engine gave it a 45 mile-per-hour road speed.[20] All tanks now had highly sophisticated fire control systems and complex armor systems.

---

[18]Hogg, *Tank Killing: Anti-Tank Warfare by Men and Machines*, 19.

[19]Ibid., 28.

[20]Citino, *Armored Forces; History and Sourcebook*, 131.

The pendulum of armor/anti-armor advantages swung back and forth repeatedly since the tank's debut in World War I, however neither side ever achieved a sustained, decisive advantage over the other. Furthermore, despite the focus on tank specific measures and countermeasures, tanks have always been vulnerable to a wide variety of non tank-specific threats, both high and low technology. Hand grenades, mines, and obstacles constitute the low-technology side, while airpower dominates the high technology side.

Precision-guided weapons from the ground and the air make armored elements more vulnerable today than ever before. The modern battlefield environment pits tanks against highly accurate and incredibly lethal weapons that diminish their survivability and effectiveness against a well-equipped adversary. Sophisticated weapons force armored elements back toward the static, defended, and concealed conditions they were designed to overcome. They cannot penetrate enemy formations unmolested in the manner their inventors envisioned them doing. Precision weapons require armored forces to be part of an overall combined arms maneuver scheme, rather than the answer in and of themselves.

Advanced precision weapons also inhibit airpower's effectiveness, but not to the same degree that they inhibit ground power's effectiveness. There are two primary reasons for the difference. First, airpower's speed and flexibility enable minimal exposure to known threats. Airpower minimizes exposure time by overflying or laterally avoiding known threat envelopes. Stealth technology enhances these exposure minimization efforts by shrinking adversary detection and engagement ranges, effectively creating larger "safe" areas in the sky. Second, airpower typically places top targeting priority on air defense systems during the opening stages of air operations. Therefore, most of an adversary's finite and considerably costly air defense assets are neutralized within days of a conflict's start. From then on, airpower operates with relative impunity over hostile territory for the remainder of the conflict.

Armor Theory

Several theorist practitioners came to the forefront during the interwar period, and their thoughts are retained in modern doctrine. J.F.C Fuller rose in Britain, along with Hans von Seeckt, Oswald Lutz, and Heinz Guderian in Germany, and Charles de Gaulle in France.

Armored doctrine took root prior to the tank's first trial at Flers and Courcellette under General Haig. Initially, theorists intended tanks to compliment and enhance infantry operations under the combined arms scheme. When E. D. Swinton released his first memorandum establishing tactical doctrine for tanks in February 1916, he stated, "tanks are an auxiliary to the infantry, that they must be counted as infantry and in operation be under the same command."[21] Early doctrine suitably considered a tank's capabilities and limitations, for its unreliability, vulnerability to artillery and machine guns, and short range prevented it from doing much more than the initial penetration it was designed to accomplish.

Swinton, the "father of the tank," saw tanks as a means to penetrate to enemy artillery but he didn't see use for tanks beside that basic purpose. He believed that tanks should be employed in mass to create a penetration, and then cavalry would exploit that initial penetration. Swinton also understood armor's vulnerability to infantry and machine guns. Therefore, he advocated two versions of tanks – a "destroyer" carrying large guns to attack artillery with large guns, and a "man-killing" tank to neutralize infantry with machine guns. Neither variant was meant to go far behind enemy lines.

J. F. C. Fuller was the first armor theorist-practitioner, having planned the first-ever tank employment at the Somme in 1916. Fuller believed that mechanized forces should almost completely replace infantry in a military force, saying "Armor can defeat the bullet; therefore a tank can replace infantry in the attack because it can ignore the fire power of infantry in the

---

[21]Swinton, *Eyewitness*, 214.

defense."[22] He envisioned future wars dominated by mechanized and motorized forces, with infantry only coming into play in terrain unsuitable for armored forces, like wooded or mountainous areas. Besides that, Fuller only saw infantry necessary to occupy previously conquered terrain.

Fuller thought the transition to an all-armor force would reduce military force numerical requirements. The new, smaller force was to be much more agile than infantry-centric forces of the past. This transition was to emphasize offensive maneuver warfare featuring armor and anti-armor forces, but it would also necessitate heavy field fortifications to protect depots along the line of operations. With this newfound mobility and operational reach, Fuller estimated Great Britain's military requirement at 30,000 perpetually mobilized men, rather than million-man armies of World War I. This was a clear plug for armored efficiency.

Charles de Gaulle was an infantryman during World War I, but he believed that tanks would revolutionize wars of the future. His thinking was very much in line with Fuller's writing: "The professional army of the future will move entirely on caterpillar wheels."[23] During the interwar period, de Gaulle influenced the French army to develop heavy tank divisions. He led the only French armored counterattack against the German invasion in 1940. Like Fuller, de Gaulle thought armored forces' efficiency would reduce the size requirements of the French army.

Hans von Seeckt led the German army's development of combined arms tactics early in the interwar period. Seeckt firmly believed in armored elements, but he did not think they could function alone like some of his contemporaries. Seeckt directed German army exercises to refine combined arms employment, and his findings were the foundation of blitzkrieg warfare.

---

[22] J. F. C. Fuller, *Armored Warfare* (Westport, CT: Greenwood Press, 1943), 45-46.

[23] Citino, *Armored Forces; History and Sourcebook*, 235.

Heinz Guderian was a key developer of the blitzkrieg concept in the German army, becoming an expert on tank tactics before he ever stepped into a tank. He is said to have read Swinton, Fuller, and de Gaulle's works to shape his own tank theories. Guderian also worked closely with Oswald Lutz to develop blitzkrieg, but Guderian gets more credit for the concept since he detailed his thought in *Achtung Panzer* in 1937.

Guderian's philosophy on armored tactics diverged from Fuller's, with the former believing strongly in tanks as the centerpiece of a combined arms force that included infantry and airpower. He also highlighted a need for fast-moving artillery that could keep pace with tanks and reposition rapidly, leading to the development of armored, self-propelled artillery. Unlike Swinton, Guderian believed armored forces could both penetrate and exploit the initial penetration when accompanied by the appropriate combined arms assets.

Guderian's keys to success were surprise, deployment en masse, and suitable terrain.[24] While he was a tireless advocate of high-tempo offensive warfare, Guderian also warned of armored forces' massive logistical requirements. This conclusion led him to advocate road network construction for use by motorized supply vehicles.

Synthesizing twentieth century heavy maneuver force theories reveals three enduring trends. First, those favoring the combined arms approach, to include infantry and airpower, found more success in actual combat. Second, the vast majority of theorists believed that armored forces would reduce the overall force requirements for conduct of war. Third, most theorists advocated high tempo offensive operations, but they also warned of the incredible logistics required for such operations. All three trends found their way into modern American heavy maneuver force doctrine, discussed below.

---

[24]Heinz Guderian, *Achtung Panzer!* trans. Christopher Duffy (London: Wellington House, 1992), 205.

Heavy Brigade Combat Team Doctrine

Modern heavy maneuver force doctrine is found in Army Field Manual 3-90.6, *The Brigade Combat Team*, and Field Manual 3-90.5, *The Combined Arms Battalion*. These two documents result from nearly a century of technological and theoretical refinement. They outline the designed capabilities and recommended employment of the modern American heavy combat forces. The following section explains the current American doctrinal approach to heavy maneuver warfare.

Heavy Brigade Combat Teams (HBCTs) wield the most combat power of any brigade in the current army organizational construct. Although every BCT includes maneuver, fires, reconnaissance, sustainment, military intelligence, military police, signal, and engineer capabilities, Heavy BCTs are the only type that contain armored elements within the maneuver and fires war fighting functions.[25] Armored elements provide the extra firepower to HBCTs over the other BCTs, but they also reduce HBCT mobility at the operational and strategic levels.

HBCTs are designed to execute combined arms operations that utilize shock and speed. According to doctrine, HBCTs' capabilities include increased firepower, mobility, and protection compared to Infantry BCTs or Stryker BCTs.[26] HBCTs leverage rapid tactical mobility to conduct penetrations and envelopments, along with screen, guard, and cover missions. With these capabilities, HBCTs seize enemy territory, destroy enemy armed forces, and eliminate the enemy's means of civil population control.[27] *The Brigade Combat Team* lists HBCT limitations as not being rapidly deployable to theater or area operations, limited capability to conduct force

---

[25]US Army, Field Manual 3-90.6, *The Brigade Combat Team* (Washington, DC: United States Department of the Army, 4 August 2006), 1-6.

[26]Ibid., 1-10.

[27]Ibid., 1-9.

entry or early entry operations, high usage rates of fuel, ammunition, and maintenance supply, and a shortfall of engineer assets to conduct gap crossings.[28]

HBCTs feature combined arms battalions (CABs) to perform their major war fighting functions. CABs use fire and maneuver to destroy or capture enemy forces, or repel their attacks by direct and indirect fire, close combat, and counterattack.[29] CABs function best in mixed and open terrain where they can maneuver and close with enemy mechanized and armor forces. According to *The Combined Arms Battalion*, CABs superior protection capabilities make them more effective than lighter battalions in high intensity conflict scenarios.

CABs perform all missions of full spectrum operations – offense, defense, stability, and security- using a two-by-two combination of armored and mechanized infantry companies. In high-intensity conflicts, CABs conduct limited penetrations, exploit success and pursue adversaries as part of a larger formation, conduct guard operations when augmented with artillery and aviation support, and combine with other formations to conduct other offensive and defensive operations.[30]

Like their parent organization, CABs face difficulties operating in urban areas, dense jungles and forests, steep and rugged terrain, and swamps and marshes.[31] They require significant amounts of strategic transportation to reach theaters of operation, and are the HBCT's primary source of demand for fuel, ammunition, and maintenance supplies. CABs are also vulnerable to mines and antitank weapons, and carry a significantly larger footprint than lighter forces. Like the HBCT, CABs lack organic gap crossing capabilities.[32]

---

[28]Ibid.

[29]US Army, Field Manual 3-90.5, *The Combined Arms Battalion* (Washington, DC: United States Department of the Army, 1 April 2008), 1-8.

[30]Ibid., 2-8.

[31]Ibid., 2-9.

[32]Ibid., 2-10.

Summary

Early tank theorists believed it possible for armored forces to return the characteristics of war from the deadlock of trench warfare back toward mobile maneuver operations. Tanks enjoyed early success in penetrating enemy lines when first employed in World War I, but anti-armor countermeasures quickly followed suit and diminished the tank's effectiveness. In the years since World War I, heavy ground maneuver forces were subject to a measure/countermeasure dynamic that gave armored elements narrow, short-lived advantages over other forces. Armor theory development recognized this dynamic and found it necessary to mix armored forces with other components, such as infantry, artillery, and airpower. Modern US Army doctrine and organization reflects armor theory, combining heavy armor forces with mechanized infantry within its CABs. Doctrine promulgates CABs as only part of a larger combined arms joint force, used to create specific effects in specific advantageous circumstances created with the help of long-range artillery and airpower. Doctrine touts the effectiveness of heavy ground maneuver forces, but advocates a wider, combined arms approach toward victory in major combat operations. Airpower, a major contributor to the combined arms scheme, is discussed in the next chapter.

Chapter 3 – Airpower Capabilities, Theory, and Doctrine

Airpower Technology

Military theorists dreamed of powered flying machines for many years prior to World War I, but the Great War catalyzed airpower's development. Rather than being conceived by a single person and then adopted by a wider audience, airpower experienced parallel development by many nations in the early twentieth century. Entrepreneurs like Samuel Langley in the United

States, and Clement Alder in France worked on flying machines prior to the turn of the century.[33] They were not alone. The British, Germans, Italians, and Russians were also developing powered aircraft around the same time.

In 1907, the U.S. Army's first specifications for a military airplane said that it should have a speed of at least forty miles per hour, be capable of carrying two persons having a combined weight of 350 pounds, and have a range of 125 miles.[34] Early aircraft barely achieved these specifications, but airpower enthusiasts continued to dream of better machines to carry out their theories.

The first documented employment of airpower in battle came on 21 October 1911, when the Italians used aircraft to reconnoiter Turkish troops in Tripoli, Libya during a war between the two states.[35] Although the unarmed aircraft were used primarily for daytime reconnaissance and artillery spotting, Italian pilots threw bombs over the side of the aircraft, and even used flashlights to attempt night reconnaissance missions. Almost immediately, military airplanes proved vulnerable to surface fires, with the first recorded battle damage from ground fire on 25 October 1911.[36]

With the race for air superiority underway, developers began mounting machine guns on aircraft prior to World War I. Antebellum aircraft, such as the British Vickers E.F.B. 1 came armed with small swivel-mounted machine guns designed to shoot other aircraft from the sky. The Vickers had a 7.7-millimeter gun, 70 mile per hour maximum speed, 4.5-hour endurance, and

---

[33]Tony Mason, *Airpower: A Centennial Approach* (London: Brassey's, 1994), 3.

[34]Francis Crosby, *A Handbook of Fighter Aircraft* (London: Anness Publishing, 2002), 10.

[35]Ibid., 11.

[36]Mason, *Airpower: A Centennial Approach*, 11.

could climb 450 feet per minute at sea level.[37] By the end of the war, aircraft such as the Sopwith Camel came armed with dual 7.7-millimeter machine guns, maximum speeds over 120 miles per hour, and climbed above 10,000 feet.

The air superiority race intensified during the interwar period, and World War II aircraft were far superior to their predecessors. At the conclusion of the war, fighter aircraft like the North American P-51 Mustang were armed with several larger caliber machine guns, bombs and rockets, and dispensable fuel tanks to increase range. They attained speeds close to 500 miles per hour, and could fly over 30,000 feet.[38] The war also hastened heavy bomber advances. One example, the Boeing B-29 flew over 30,000 feet at 365 miles per hour, carried a formidable assortment of self-defense machine guns, and carried 20,000 pounds of bombs.[39] Of note, B-29s performed the first-ever atomic weapon deliveries on Hiroshima and Nagasaki in 1945.

Just like armor, airpower advances inspired daunting countermeasures during World War II. Bomber crews had amongst the highest casualty rates of any specialty in the war. Radar replaced observers to warn of airborne attacks, and anti-aircraft artillery became increasingly lethal. Guns experienced significantly increased rates of fire, larger calibers, improved ballistics, and high-explosive airburst shells. Combined with radar and height finding equipment, these guns leveled the playing field with military aircraft.

Jet-propelled aircraft entered the scene at the end of the war, with the German Messerschmitt ME-262 starting production in 1944.[40] The ME-262 aircraft sparked a technological revolution that continues today. Jets experienced continual refinements throughout

---

[37]William Green and Gordon Swanborough, *The Complete Book of Fighters* (New York: Barnes and Noble Books, 1998), 574.

[38]Ibid., 448.

[39]Boeing, History, "B-29 Superfortress," http://www.boeing.com/history/boeing/ b29.html (accessed 16 May 2011).

[40]Green and Swanborough, *The Complete Book of Fighters*, 382.

the 1950s in both fighter and bomber aircraft, and they dominated modern air forces by the end of the decade. Jet fighters gained heat seeking air-to-air missiles, aircraft-mounted radars, and radar-guided air-to-air missiles. Increased speed and altitude capabilities reduced their vulnerability to surface-fired weapons.

Perhaps one of the most important airpower developments did not directly involve fighter or bomber aircraft – aerial refueling. General Carl Spaatz made in-flight refueling the newly formed U.S. Air Force's top priority when he assumed the Chief of Staff role in 1947. After a rapid development process, a B-29 flew non-stop around the world in ninety-four hours from 26 February to 3 March 1949, refueling in-flight three times along the way.[41] This achievement marked a quantum leap in airpower's operational reach.

Precision guided munitions (PGM) were the second key development in airpower effectiveness and efficiency. Originally developed during the Vietnam conflict, PGMs captured public attention during Operation Desert Storm in 1991. Although PGMs comprised only 10 percent of the total bombs dropped during the war, they were far more effective than their unguided counterparts.[42] Laser-guided PGMs, and their accompanying infrared targeting pods increased weapon accuracy, night delivery capability, and reconnaissance abilities. By the late 1990s Global Positioning System (GPS)-guided weapons added an all-weather precision capability.

Anti-aircraft capabilities have also increased over the decades, following the same measure-countermeasure pattern as for heavy ground forces. Surface-to-air missiles followed closely behind jet aircraft, and missile range and lethality has improved markedly over the last fifty years. Anti-aircraft range, lethality, and cueing systems also experienced significant

---

[41]*Flight Magazine*, "A Girdle Round the Earth," 10 March 1949, http://www.flightglobal.com/pdfarchive/view/1949/1949%20-%200461.html (accessed 16 May 2011).

[42]Elliot A. Cohen and Thomas A. Kearney, *Gulf War Air Power Survey, Summary Report* (Washington, DC: United States Department of the Air Force, 1993), 12.

enhancement to compliment missile improvements. Stealth technology is now twenty years old, and is commonplace in modern military design.

Trends emerge from the technological realm of airpower. Aircraft today fly much faster, higher, and further than their ancestors from the turn of the twentieth century. Today's airpower weapons are far more lethal and accurate than weapons of the past. Anti-aircraft measures are also more lethal and precise, but stealth technology diminishes countermeasure effectiveness. All of these developments drive the price of airpower up exponentially. The aircraft that cost a few thousand dollars in World War II now cost hundreds of millions of dollars, or in some cases, multi-billion dollars.

Airpower Theory

Giulio Douhet is widely recognized as the father of airpower theory. The Italian airpower theorist became enamored with airpower the first time he witnessed an Italian dirigible in flight in 1905. He firmly believed that airpower was the key component of military strength in future wars, famously writing, "To have command of the air means to be in a position to wield offensive power so great it defies human imagination. It means to be able to cut an enemy's army and navy off from their bases of operation and nullify their chances of winning the war."[43] Like with Swinton's vision of armored warfare, Douhet foresaw capabilities and employment of airpower before technology could accomplish his vision.

Douhet argued that airpower was an unstoppable, inherently offensive weapon that could strike enemy vital centers with a combination of explosive, incendiary, and poison gas weapons.[44] Vital centers included industrial and commercial establishments, important public and private buildings, transportation arteries and centers, and certain designated areas of civilian

---

[43]Giulio Douhet, *The Command of the Air*, trans. Dino Ferrari (Washington, DC: Office of Air Force History, 1983), 23.

[44]Ibid., 20.

population.[45] Such attacks, Douhet believed, would smash "the material and moral resources of a people caught up in a frightful cataclysm which haunts them everywhere without cease until the final collapse of all social organization."[46] In essence, Douhet advocated direct attacks on civilian populations to crush an enemy's will to wage war.

According to Douhet, these direct attacks against the enemy's will produced quick, decisive results that reduced bloodshed and made war more humane in the long run. He believed that airpower's characteristics of speed, surprise, and flexibility held any target at risk while making ground forces obsolete. In Douhet's mind, these airpower characteristics could also save the world from another trench warfare stalemate like what occurred in World War I. Douhet was history's first airpower theorist, and also the first to hint at airpower's efficiency. With his assumption of airpower's primacy as a strategic, offensive weapon, he saw it necessary to create a separate, independent air component, led by airmen.

Hugh Trenchard, the first Royal Air Force commander, also saw airpower as the means to break the enemy's will. Having experienced the German bombings on London during World War I, he had firsthand experience of airpower's psychological effect on public morale. He advocated targeting the civilian population, though less directly than was promoted by Douhet. Trenchard believed that attacks on industry alone would break civilian morale without targeting civilians directly. He got somewhat more specific than Douhet, naming iron and coal mines, steel mills, chemical production facilities, explosive factories, aero engine and magneto works, submarine and shipbuilding works, large gun foundries, and engine repair shops as airpower's primary targets.[47]

---

[45]Ibid.

[46]Ibid., 61.

[47]Phillip S. Meilinger, *Airmen and Air Theory: A Review of the Sources* (Maxwell Air Force Base, AL: Air University Press, 2001), 118.

Like Douhet, Hugh Trenchard viewed airpower as a strategic, offensive weapon that should be used to attack strategic enemy assets far behind the front lines. He also saw the importance of obtaining airpower first before any other effort. Unlike Douhet, Trenchard did not necessarily believe that air efforts should be separated from ground efforts. He might have lacked the vision of Douhet to see airpower's future capabilities that had not yet developed. He did not think that airpower could be decisive in and of itself, but rather could set conditions for ground forces to advance and occupy enemy territory.

John Slessor was one of Hugh Trenchard's bright young officers in the Royal Air Force, and he was the first notable airpower theorist that began his career as an aviator. His views departed somewhat from the previous theorists. Slessor viewed airpower more closely aligned with ground efforts than did Douhet or Trenchard. He believed that airpower could not be decisive by itself, for strategic strikes would not affect a war as quickly as was necessary. Slessor believed that air and ground efforts needed to be closely coordinated in a collaborative effort throughout the duration of a conflict.

Slessor was also the first to articulate the concept of parallel operations in air combat. He believed that airpower could conduct multiple operations simultaneously, such as maintaining air superiority and interdicting enemy surface targets.[48] With this in mind, he pushed toward ground supply interdiction as a way to culminate enemy forces in contact with friendly elements on the front lines. Slessor worried about coordination for airpower in tactical roles, but he managed to describe air support to friendly breakthrough efforts, pursuits, and defending against enemy breakthroughs.

William "Billy" Mitchell was the outspoken American airpower theorist whose ideas laid the foundation of modern US Air Force doctrine. Mitchell developed his airpower concepts as a World War I aviator, and also through his relationship with Hugh Trenchard. Those ideas did not

---

[48]Ibid., 65.

stray far from Trenchard's or Giulio Douhet's, who Mitchell is said to have met with during a conference in 1922.[49] Although originally a proponent of airpower to support ground offensives, Mitchell grew to believe that airpower could be a much more humane way to wage war than fighting it out in the trenches, a lesson he learned from his experiences in World War I.

Like his contemporaries, Mitchell believed that airpower would be the dominant force in future conflicts. Mitchell's sentiments echoed Douhet's, with emphasis on destroying an enemy's air force, maintaining air superiority throughout a conflict, and using bombers to attack the enemy's vital centers. Like Douhet, Mitchell thought air attacks on vital centers at war's outset would result in "diminished loss of life and treasure and will thus be a distinct benefit to civilization,"[50] another advertisement for airpower's efficiency. Mitchell believed strongly in airpower's defensive capabilities as well, demonstrated when he sank a captured German battleship off the Virginia coast in 1921.

Mitchell was perhaps most famous for advocating a separate air service of equal stature to the US Army and Navy. Although he promoted both tactical and strategic missions, Mitchell thought strategic bombing missions would ultimately decide future wars. He went so far as to say that an independent air force could win future wars without the help of any surface component. With so much importance on the strategic component, Mitchell believed that air operations could only be planned and led by air-minded officers. Mitchell's philosophy served to inspire many of the airpower theorists that emerged in the interwar period, most notably the members of the Air Corps Tactical School who drove air war planning efforts prior to World War II.

The Air Corps Tactical School had many influential personalities that rose in the Army Air Corps ranks, and later formed the nucleus of the US Air Force. Drawing from its predecessors, the Tactical School believed, "The most efficient way to defeat an enemy is to

---

[49]Ibid., 92.

[50]Mitchell, *Winged Defense*, 16.

destroy, by means of bombardment from the air, his war-making capacity; the means to this end is to identify by scientific analysis those particular elements of his war potential the elimination of which will cripple either his war machine or his will to continue the conflict."[51] This indicated a systematic approach toward attacking specific nodes of an adversary's vital centers in order to end a conflict without significant ground operations. In fact the Tactical School believed ground operations were only necessary if, by chance, the air offensive did not prove conclusive.[52]

This philosophy led to the development of Air War Plans Division One (AWPD-1), the World War II air war plan that former members of the Tactical School drafted in 1941. Under AWPD-1, air planners examined the German military system to define its most critical and most vulnerable nodes that could not be replaced on short order. The result plan included 154 targets divided into four broad categories – electric power facilities, transportation, synthetic petroleum production, and the Luftwaffe.[53] AWPD-1 advocated high altitude precision daylight bombing to destroy the targets. It identified the first three categories as primary objectives, but made the Luftwaffe, or obtaining air superiority, an essential intermediate objective to enable those primary objectives.

Clearly, AWPD-1 and the bombing operations it drove did not achieve the decisive effect the Tactical School planners hoped for. While bombing operations did successfully destroy many targets off the list, the war dragged on for years and the Air Corps suffered massive losses. Victory did not come until the combined effort of ground and air forces wore Axis forces down. Although not completely successful, the "vital centers" approach dominated airpower doctrine for decades after the war. It was not until John Boyd, influenced by scientific theories regarding chaos and uncertainty, that airpower theory significantly changed.

---

[51]Barry D. Watts, *The Foundations of US Air Doctrine: The Problem of Friction in War* (Maxwell Air Force Base, AL: Air University Press, 1984), 18.

[52]Ibid., 19.

[53]Ibid.

John Boyd was a Korea War-era fighter pilot that built his famous Observation-Orientation-Decision-Action cycle, or OODA loop, from combat experience gained against Soviet MiG jets in the skies over Korea. Boyd originally built the OODA loop to address aerial combat techniques, but later adopted the loop to fit operational and strategic war scenarios. Similar to his predecessors, Boyd believed in strategic bombing, but he introduced the concept of strategic paralysis to win wars.

The strategic paralysis approach viewed the enemy as complex, adaptive system operating in a dynamic environment. Boyd's approach maintained his predecessors' strategic emphasis, but Boyd shifted the focus of strategic targeting. Under strategic paralysis, war fighters attack enemy sustainment and control capabilities in order to "collapse adversary's system into confusion and disorder by causing him to over and under react to activity that appears simultaneously menacing as well as ambiguous, chaotic, and misleading."[54] Boyd also departed from his airpower theory forerunners by advocating the goal of subduing the enemy without fighting, rather than previous attrition and annihilation strategies.

John Warden was a Boyd disciple who gained notoriety for planning the air portion of Operation Desert Storm while working at the US Air Force's Checkmate think tank organization in 1990. Warden promulgated airpower as the dominant fighting element of twenty-first century conflict, touting its unmatchable utility in the strategic realm. Warden's "five strategic rings" model took a prescriptive approach to defeating an adversary by directly attacking his leadership.

Warden used three main ways to defeat adversary leadership – coercion, incapacitation, and annihilation. This approach blends thoughts from most of the previous airpower theorists. The coercion aspect aimed to break the enemy's will to resist by exceeding that enemy's pain

---

[54]John R. Boyd, "Patterns of Conflict" (Briefing, December 1986), http://www.ausairpower.net/JRB/poc.pdf (accessed 19 August 2011), 7.

threshold violently and instantaneously through simultaneous and parallel attacks.[55] Incapacitation, or paralysis strategy, approached strategic attack in the same fashion as John Boyd. Finally, annihilation sought to destroy the entire system, making enemy leadership irrelevant, however, Warden acknowledged that the annihilation strategy would rarely, if ever, be politically acceptable.

In summary, airpower theory from its earliest days to the present tends to focus on strategic and operational-level effects. Airpower theory exploits airpower's speed, surprise, and flexibility to bypass enemy fielded forces and strike directly at adversary vital interests. While earlier theory concentrated on physical infrastructure such as factories or centers of population, more recent doctrine advocates strategic paralysis by attacking enemy leadership and the networks between leadership and fielded forces.

Airpower Doctrine

Modern airpower doctrine regarding major combat operations is found in Air Force Doctrine Document 1, *Air Force Basic Doctrine*, and Air Force Doctrine Document 3-03, *Counterland Operations*. Like the Army doctrine publications, these two doctrine documents describe airpower's capabilities and recommended employment. This section provides a brief overview of each publication's content and central arguments.

Air Force Basic Doctrine lists seven tenets, or fundamental truths, concerning the application of air and space power. Each tenet is traceable back to the influential airpower theorists discussed in the previous section. The tenets are: that airpower should be centrally controlled and de-centrally executed; airpower is flexible and versatile; airpower produces synergistic effects; airpower offers a unique form of persistence; airpower must achieve

---

[55]Phillip S. Meilinger, *The Paths of Heaven: The Evolution of Airpower Theory* (Maxwell Air Force Base, AL: Air University Press, 1997), 375.

concentration of purpose; airpower must be prioritized; and airpower must be balanced.[56] Two tenets – flexibility/versatility, and synergy – are particularly relevant for comparison to heavy ground maneuver forces.

According to *Air Force Basic Doctrine*, flexibility allows airpower to exploit mass and maneuver simultaneously by quickly shifting from one campaign objective to another.[57] With flexibility, air planners can shift objectives either from one sortie to the next, or re-roll missions in flight. Versatility means that airpower applies simultaneously at the strategic, operational, and tactical levels of war. Versatility brings airpower to bear in parallel operations that present adversaries with multiple simultaneous crises so they cannot deal with all, or sometimes, any of the crises.[58]

Air Force Basic Doctrine defines synergy as airpower's ability to generate coordinated, parallel attacks which produce effects that exceed the contributions of forces employed individually.[59] Coordinated attacks bring disproportionate effects on the enemy system to comply with our political will. Synergy, combined with flexibility and versatility enable airpower to react quickly and appropriately to adversary actions.

The Air Force foundational doctrine publication also lists seventeen key operational functions. The most relevant functions to this discussion are strategic attack, counterair, counterland, and surveillance and reconnaissance. *Air Force Basic Doctrine* says that airpower is inherently a strategic and offensive force that can simultaneously threaten all of the enemy's instruments of power.[60] Strategic attack includes missions directed specifically against enemy

---

[56]US Air Force, Air Force Doctrine Document (AFDD) 1, *Air Force Basic Doctrine* (Washington, DC: United States Department of the Air Force, 17 November 2003), 27.

[57]Ibid., 30.

[58]Ibid.

[59]Ibid., 31.

[60]Ibid., 41.

leadership, to either destroy that leadership or separate it from its fielded forces. Counterair involves missions dedicated to preserving freedom of action for friendly air and ground forces.

Air Force doctrine breaks counterland into two primary missions – air interdiction, and close air support. *Air Force Basic Doctrine* introduces the two mission types, but *Counterland Operations* discusses both missions in much greater detail. Air interdiction includes deep attacks intended to delay, disrupt, or destroy enemy forces behind the front lines, before their combat power can be employed against friendly ground forces. *Counterland Operations* highlight several interdiction effects, including channeling enemy movements, constricting the enemy logistics system, disrupting enemy communications, forcing urgent movement upon the enemy, and attrition of the enemy.[61] The air component doctrine typically supports shaping operations for ground maneuver elements with interdiction missions, but the air component may also be the supported element when directly prosecuting Joint Force Commander objectives.

Close air support targets enemy assets in close proximity to friendly forces, requiring detailed integration to coordinate fires and prevent fratricide. It is prioritized to destroy, suppress, neutralize, disrupt, fix, or delay the most threatening enemy elements.[62] Doctrine lists close air support effects as facilitating ground action and inducing shock, disruption, and disorder against enemy forces. Doctrine also warns that while CAS is effective, it is not the most efficient use of airpower due to the extensive planning, coordination, and control required.[63]

Summary

Like armor theorists, air theorists believed that airpower could revolutionize the characteristics of war, providing a quicker, more efficient, and comparatively humane result.

---

[61]US Air Force, Air Force Doctrine Document (AFDD) 3-03, *Counterland Operations* (Washington, DC: United States Department of the Air Force, 17 September 2010), 21.

[62]Ibid., 33.

[63]US Air Force, Air Force Doctrine Document (AFDD) 3-1, *Air Warfare* (Washington, DC: United States Department of the Air Force, 17 September 2010), 12.

Early theorists sought to use airpower to bypass an adversary's front line forces and attack directly at his vital centers – in varying combinations including population, industry, transportation, and leadership. Later, theory shifted towards attacking critical connections between vital centers in order to disorganize, disrupt, and defeat an adversary. Airpower theory drove development of precision-guided munitions designed to attack pinpoint targets deep behind enemy lines in order to produce decisive results as quickly as possible. Over the years, airpower weapon systems gained range, speed, maneuverability, and precision – all fundamental characteristics of airpower that shape modern doctrine. Current Air Force doctrine leverages airpower's characteristics to promote precision engagement via strategic attack, air interdiction, and close air support in order to support war-fighting efforts. It echoes the early theorists' views that airpower is most efficient when operating independently of ground forces.

Chapter 4 – Comparison

Airpower and heavy ground power feature similar yet diverse characteristics employed by military practitioners in the conduct of operational art. The following model displays the characteristics, functions, tasks, and missions that shape the way each force is employed in war. The model is derived from each force's respective theory and doctrine that were outlined above.

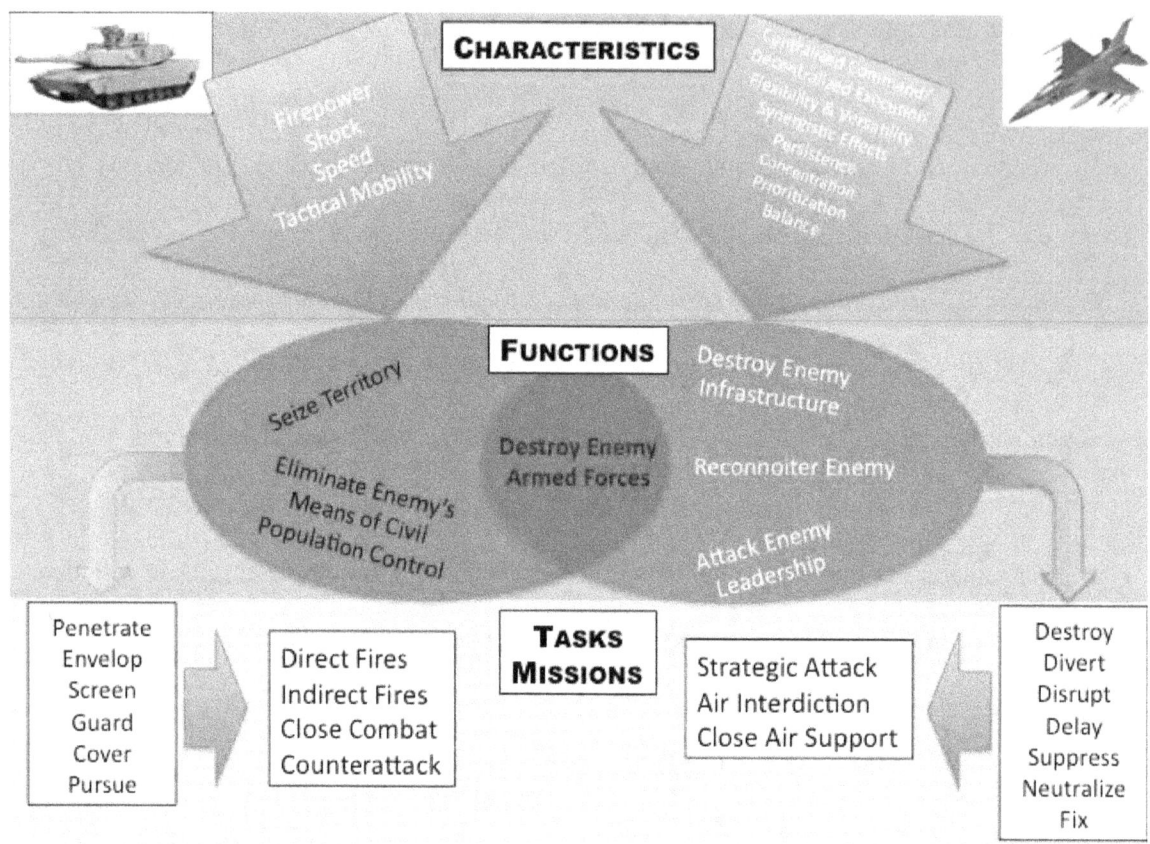

Figure 1: Airpower/Heavy Ground Power Comparison Model

Source: Created by author.

The model begins with the characteristics, or attributes, of each force as described in their

respective doctrine documents. Army doctrine lists firepower, shock, speed, and tactical mobility

as the fundamental attributes that characterize armored forces, while Air Force doctrine list the

seven tenets of centralized control/decentralized execution, flexibility and versatility, synergistic

effects, persistence, concentration, prioritization, and balance as basic attributes that are unique to

airpower. These characteristics feed into the capabilities, or functions, that each force can

perform.

Functions in the model also stem from the services' doctrine and relevant theory that

applies to modern forces. According to Army doctrine, heavy ground forces can destroy enemy armed forces, seize terrain, and eliminate the enemy's means of civil population control. Meanwhile, combat airpower can destroy enemy armed forces, destroy enemy infrastructure, attack enemy leadership, and reconnoiter the enemy. As the model shows, destroying enemy armed forces is the only overlapping function of air and heavy ground combat power. These functions may also be considered capabilities, and they enable the tasks that each force performs.

The tasks, powered by capabilities, that are listed in the model also stem from each service's respective doctrine. On the ground, heavy combat forces can penetrate, envelop, screen, guard, cover, and pursue enemy forces. Airpower can divert, destroy, disrupt, delay, suppress, neutralize, or fix the adversary. Evidenced by the task diversity, each force component contributes to joint operational art in different ways.

The ways are articulated through the missions listed in doctrine. Ways illustrate how each force's characteristics come to fruition in battle. For example, airpower delays enemy forces through air interdiction missions against enemy infrastructure and close air support missions targeting enemy fielded forces. Similarly, heavy ground forces penetrate adversary defensive belts through direct fires, indirect fires, and close combat missions. These missions can be complimentary when appropriately planned and coordinated by operational artists.

Summary

A quick look at the model reveals very distinct differences between airpower and heavy ground combat power. The differences stem from the inherent characteristics of the machines that comprise each force component, and they filter through functions on to tasks and missions that each force component provides to the operational artist. There is only one overlapping function between airpower and heavy ground power- destruction of enemy forces- and the two force components leverage their fundamental characteristics in very different ways to perform that function.

The model shows why and how each combat element performs tasks and missions outlined in its doctrine. Operational artists must understand how each force component derives its combat power for the specific roles it is doctrinally obligated to fill. Thorough understanding of the concepts behind the model should ensure that each component is employed in appropriate and favorable conditions. Favorable employment translates to increased effectiveness and efficiency on the battlefield, a concept discussed in the next chapter.

Chapter 5 – Efficiency, Effectiveness, and Efficacy

As mentioned in the introduction, military practitioners are commonly accused of preferring effectiveness to efficiency in conduct of war. The stakes in war are too high, and the uncertainty is too great to risk applying only the minimum force required to prevail without an 'Option B' branch plan if the primary plan fails. 'Option B' usually means bringing far greater force to bear against the enemy than minimally necessary for victory, with offensive force ratios ranging anywhere from 3:1 to 6:1. Additionally, planners build reserve forces to reinforce the main effort if that overwhelming mass somehow fails. Such overwhelming mass ensures victory, but it is not remotely efficient. At the end of conflict however, effectiveness is what truly matters to military and political leaders. That is, of course, until budget constraints come into play and military expenditures begin to tip the balance of national power. Efficacy becomes an important concept when constraints gain influence on the military,

The concept of efficacy captures the middle ground between efficiency and effectiveness in the all-or-nothing realm of military conflict. Efficacy refers to the capacity for producing a desired result or effect. In the context of war, efficacy means the degree to which a force can achieve victory. It blends the concepts of ensuring results while conducting operations as inexpensively as possible. Although the former two terms are most frequently used to measure military operations, practitioners are truly searching for efficacy in their craft.

Efficacy is most closely related to the principle of economy of force, originally coined by Clausewitz, which remains in the military lexicon today. In his chapter on economy of force, Clausewitz wrote, "If a segment of one's force is located where it is not sufficiently busy with the enemy . . . then these forces are being managed uneconomically. In this sense, they are being wasted, which is even worse than using them inappropriately."[64] Army FM 3-0, *Operations* interprets economy of force to mean accepting prudent risks in selected areas to achieve superiority in the decisive operation.[65] The Air Force doctrinal definition is similar, prescribing maximum effort toward primary objectives while secondary efforts receive only the minimum essential resources.[66]

J. F. C. Fuller believed so strongly in economy of force that he defined it as the central law of war in which all other principles were based. His nine principles, which are closely related to the modern American principles of war, all focused around attaining economy of force. Fuller tied also economy of force to technology, stating, "At the base of every new invention we find economy written in capital letters."[67] He recognized the advantages of technology but also acknowledged technology's limitations, manifested by countermeasures and the laws of war.

Strategist Edward Luttwak also discussed the relationship between technology and efficiency in *Strategy: The Logic of War and Peace.* Luttwak states, "Dramatic increases in efficiency can be obtained only by replacing generic equipment built to do many things at varying levels of efficiency with much more specialized equipment built to produce one output altogether

---

[64]Carl Von Clausewitz, *On War*, ed. and trans. Michael Howard and Peter Paret (Princeton, NJ: Princeton University Press, 1976), 213.

[65]US Army, Field Manual 3-0, *Operations*, Change 1 (Washington, DC: United States Department of the Army, February 2011), A-2.

[66]US Air Force, Air Force Doctrine Document (AFDD) 1, *Air Force Basic Doctrine* (Washington, DC: United States Department of the Air Force, 17 November 2003), 113.

[67]J. F. C. Fuller, *Foundations of Science and War* (repr., Fort Leavenworth, KS: U.S. Army Command and General Staff College Press, 1990), http://www.cgsc.edu/carl/ resources/csi/fuller2/fuller2.asp#194 (accessed 19 August 2011).

more efficiently."[68] These dramatic increases in efficiency can greatly alter the equilibrium of military power.

Tanks are the perfect example of a purpose-built machine that dramatically increased the efficiency of ground forces and shifted the balance of power during World War I. The tank enabled contextually small groups of soldiers to achieve penetrations across otherwise impregnable defensive measures. Previous penetration attempts without tanks cost both sides tens of thousands of lives. The only problem was that tanks' specialized advantage was short lived as countermeasures emerged, rendering tanks nearly as vulnerable as any other vehicle on the battlefield.

Luttwak calls countermeasure development the reciprocal force-development effect.[69] He argues that broadly capable systems prevail over specialized systems to cut short the latter's span of success. In many cases, the reciprocal force-development effect gives even greater capabilities to the versatile system that the specialized system was designed to defeat, rendering that specialized system obsolete. While their many countermeasures did not render tanks obsolete, they certainly reduced the armored advantage, and many of the countermeasure systems had wider ranging capabilities. The 88-milimeter gun is a perfect example. It could neutralize tanks and defend vital areas against enemy air attacks.

Summary

The previous chapters illustrated that military forces operate with the greatest degree of efficacy when they are employed in circumstances that play to their strengths. Airpower is most productive when operating independently of ground forces where little coordination is required and fratricide concerns are low. Heavy ground power is most effective when used against inferior

---

[68]Edward N. Luttwak, *Strategy: The Logic of War and Peace* (Cambridge, MA: Harvard University Press, 1987), 34.

[69]Ibid., 35.

adversaries that possess lesser firepower and fewer anti-armor capabilities. Efficacy diminishes when either force component is employed outside of these favorable conditions. Unfavorable circumstances may be unavoidable at times, but operational artists should seek to minimize the occurrence of such conditions. Careful planning and situation management promotes economy of force, in turn allowing each force component to operate at maximum efficacy.

Chapter 6 – Case Studies

The model displayed above shows the characteristics that contribute to airpower and heavy ground power capabilities, and it shows that those capabilities are converted into tasks and then assembled into missions. The model illustrates how each force component's characteristics drive that component toward greater efficacy in specific conditions. Operational planners must strive to set those conditions that promote efficacy for each force component. The monograph now moves to case study analysis to examine how ground and airpower's efficacies were enhanced or constricted in specific circumstances. The case studies highlight specific evidence of the two force components' employment in battle to draw conclusions about each force's efficacy.

The case study analysis examines major combat operations during the two recent conflicts in Iraq, Operation Desert Storm (ODS) and Operation Iraqi Freedom (OIF). Both operations took place in the same, mostly permissive operational environment that included open desert and relatively limited urban, wooded, or mountainous terrain, with generally clear weather conditions. ODS and OIF major combat operations also featured similarly equipped force components. Being separated by only 12 years, only minor technological refinements differentiated each fighting force, and there was no major technological revolution or revolution in military affairs between the two conflicts.

There were, however, differences between the adversary and political objectives between the two wars. ODS featured a strong opponent whose objective was to execute a quick land grab in order to pay off national debts. Coalition objectives were to expel Iraqi forces from Kuwait, restore the international border, and preserve Kuwaiti sovereignty and regional stability. These conditions favored an air war since coalition objectives did not require extensive territorial occupation. OIF, on the other hand, featured a weakened adversary who fought for survival. Coalition objectives were to remove and replace the regime with a new government that was more amiable toward western influence. The nature of the adversary and political objectives in OIF put more weight on heavy ground forces to achieve the strategic aims. This close combat environment required efficacy in ground forces while hampering the efficacy of air forces.

Operation Desert Storm

Operation Desert Storm consisted of a 43-day air operation followed by a four-day ground operation. It featured the Air Force's first attempt at strategic paralysis via a supported air operation. The air operations plan, built by the Air Force's Checkmate strategic studies group, was a vast departure the United States Central Command's draft operations plan (OPLAN) 1002-90 *Defense of the Arabian Peninsula*.[70] OPLAN 1002-90 was rooted in 1986's AirLand Battle doctrine, and it called for a defensive, attrition-based posture, trading space for time until sufficient forces were built up to conduct a counter attack and recapture lost terrain. The realized plan featured parallel attacks that struck Iraqi infrastructure, air defense, leadership, command and control nodes, and fielded forces simultaneously. It resulted in a four-phase operation that included: Phase I – Strategic Attacks, Phase II – Suppressing Enemy Air Defenses in the Kuwaiti Theater of Operations, Phase III – Preparation of the Battlefield, and Phase IV – Ground Operations. The operation marked the first time in history that the air component was the supported command for the first three phases of a conflict.

---

[70]Cohen and Kearney, *Gulf War Air Power Survey, Summary Report*, 8.

Expecting heavy losses, political and military leaders built up coalition forces to over 660,000 personnel deployed into theater before the outset of hostilities.[71] This force was realized to be excessive by the end of the war. Coalition forces included roughly 1,800 combat aircraft of all types matched up against 700 Iraqi combat aircraft, 60 anti-aircraft missile batteries and close to 3,000 anti-aircraft guns.[72] The air component flew between 2,000 and 3,000 sorties per day for most of the war. Ground forces were comparably matched against 5,000 Iraqi tanks, 3,900 armored personnel carriers, 300 multiple rocket launch systems, 350 self-propelled guns, 3,500 towed guns, and roughly 540,000 Iraqi personnel.[73] In both air and ground weapon systems, coalition technology far exceeded Iraqi technology.

Airpower methodically deconstructed and disorganized the Iraqi military system and heavy ground power advanced rapidly and decisively deep into Iraqi territory. Initial attacks focused on airfields, the integrated air defense system, leadership command and control systems, scud missile sites, nuclear, chemical, and biological weapon production sites, and electric power plants.[74] The war also demonstrated the first widespread use of precision-guided munitions (PGM) in warfare. Although PGM only accounted for slightly more than 10 percent of the total bombs dropped, they made a significant impact on the outcome of the conflict, mitigating damage and casualties on both sides of the war.

Phase I began on 17 January 1991 with strategic attacks against the Iraqi political and military system. Planners exploited PGM and stealth technology to neutralize and destroy leadership, command and control, air defense, and nuclear, chemical and biological weapon target

---

[71]Department of Defense, *Conduct of the Persian Gulf Conflict: Final Report to Congress* (Washington, DC: Government Printing Office, 1992), 86.

[72]Cohen and Kearney, *Gulf War Air Power Survey, Summary Report*, 8.

[73]Thomas Houlahan, *Gulf War: The Complete History* (New London, NH: Schrenker Military Publishing, 1999), 26.

[74]Cohen and Kearney, *Gulf War Air Power Survey, Summary Report*, 11.

sets. They also targeted known fixed Scud missile sites in order to minimize the war's political effects outside of Iraq, such as in nearby Israel. Meanwhile, air planners simultaneously orchestrated parallel attacks against the Iraqi air force facilities and assets, as well as Iraqi fielded forces during the strategic attack phase. This marked the beginning of Phase II operations, and began nearly simultaneously with the Phase I efforts. Air operations were so effective that by 26 January, Iraqis began flying the remnants of their air force to Iran and hiding airplanes in populated areas to prevent their destruction.

Once airpower neutralized the Phase I and Phase II target sets, the air planners shifted focus to Iraqi fielded forces in Kuwait, but also targeted Iraqi infrastructure. Planners targeted critical road infrastructure like bridges with remaining PGMs, and targeted troop concentrations with unguided antipersonnel weapons and anti-armor weapons. During these Phase III operations, planners also discovered the effectiveness of PGMs against enemy armor formations, and aircrew began the practice of what later became known as "tank plinking."

The Iraqis attempted their only ground attack of the war on 30 January 1991, using the 5th Mechanized Division against Khafji in Saudi Arabia during the coalition's Phase III operations.[75] Once discovered, air planners immediately shifted 140 tactical aircraft to the area, destroying nearly the division's entire lead armored brigade by the end of the day. Air planners resumed normal operations with this division completely neutralized. Airpower was said to have disrupted the Khafji battle before it started. Days before the attack, coalition intelligence intercepted radio communications indicating the Iraqi III Corps scheduled a planning conference. Coalition targeteers scanned the area for probable locations for such a meeting, and within hours air strikes launched against the most likely meeting site. The resulting attack killed a large portion

---

[75]Elliot A. Cohen, *Gulf War Air Power Survey, Volume II: Operations and Effects and Effectiveness* (Washington, DC: United States Department of the Air Force, 1993), 273.

of III Corps leadership.[76] This example highlighted airpower's flexibility and versatility, centralized control/decentralized execution, and concentration tenets during the war.

General Schwarzkopf, the coalition forces commander, desired 50 percent attrition of Iraqi forces, across the board, prior to commencement of ground operations. Although there was much consternation over battle damage assessment values, by 22 February 1991, two days before ground operations began, leaders generally agreed on the numbers that they reported to American civilian leadership. They reported that twenty-two of Iraq's forty-three divisions were less than 75 percent combat effective, with eleven of those divisions below 50 percent.[77] Two Republican Guard divisions remained fully intact, with the rest between 55 percent and 88 percent effective.[78]

Phase IV, the ground operation, began on 24 February 1991 with the VII Corps' armored penetration from the south and the XVIII Airborne Corps' famous "left hook" from the west. VII Corps relied on its Abrams tanks to penetrate Iraqi minefields at the beginning of its move northward. Armored forces continued to lead the ground effort and protect the flanks while coalition forces destroyed some Iraqi elements and forced the rest to withdraw. Meanwhile airpower conducted interdiction and close air support missions to support and protect the friendly advance. Different elements applied airpower in varied ways. VII Corps tended to utilize airpower for deep battle as doctrinally described in 1986's Army Field Manual 100-5 *Air Land Battle*, while Marine units that had less organic firepower relied on airpower more for close air support missions.[79]

Analysts noted that airpower had difficulty striking stationary vehicles during Phase IV. Despite the open desert conditions, pilots found it challenging to locate vehicles without large

---

[76]Houlahan, *Gulf War: The Complete History*, 68.

[77]Cohen, *Gulf War Air Power Survey, Volume II*, 284.

[78]Ibid.

[79]Ibid., 310.

dust trails generated by movement or JSTARS aircraft cueing. The JSTARS also relied on motion to detect enemy vehicles. Once vehicles moved, either directly fleeing coalition forces or avoiding contact altogether, airpower yielded devastating effects. It took heavy force contact, or threat of contact to get those enemy vehicles moving.

President Bush called for a cease-fire four days after ground operations began, with the air and ground joint effort having driven Iraqi forces out of Kuwait and destroying a significant portion of Iraqi combat capability.

Assessment

It is difficult, if not impossible, to precisely measure airpower's impact on the first Gulf War. Clearly, new developments like stealth and PGM made a huge difference on the war's outcome. Many effects were qualitatively measurable, but not quantifiably measurable, and that muddied the overall ability calculate each force component's effectiveness in the war.

For example, it is known that Iraqi air force assets either fled to Iran or were dispersed into centers of population by 26 January 1991, nine days after air operations commenced. Therefore, historians can pinpoint the day that the Iraqi Air Force completely ceased to function, but it is hard to calculate exactly how many pieces of equipment were destroyed. Another example was the Iraqi tank crews that feared airpower so badly that they refused to remain inside their vehicles. Although one particular tank may not have been destroyed, it became combat ineffective due to the psychological effect of airpower on the tank crews. Such an effect is all but impossible to quantify.

The second problem with effectiveness calculation was the contention over battle damage assessments between airpower and ground power. Constant disagreement occurred about which targets airpower destroyed and which targets ground power destroyed. Such disagreement was evident even inside the same ground unit when one battalion commander from 2d Armor Division believed airpower destroyed very few Iraqi armor pieces along his axis of advance. The G-3 from the very same brigade believed airpower destroyed most of the armor in his brigade's area of operations.[80] Disagreements like this typified the battle damage assessment process during ODS, so it remains difficult to definitively attribute combat victories to one combat element or the other.

It can be assessed that both airpower and heavy ground displayed tremendous efficacy in ODS. Coalition forces achieved their objectives with far fewer losses to aircraft and personnel than initially estimated. Both force components operated in conditions that favored efficacy. The air component enjoyed forty-three days of strategic attack and air interdiction without having to do significant coordination with the ground component. Heavy ground forces got to fight against a weakened and disorganized adversary that could not counter the speed and firepower of coalition tanks and artillery. Both forces benefitted from the favorable environmental conditions that made targeting and maneuver relatively simple.

Operation Iraqi Freedom

Operation Iraqi Freedom, although fought on the same terrain, marked a very different operational approach from ODS. The war's context was much different than its predecessor's from just over a decade earlier. OIF featured a comparably smaller coalition force of only 340,000 personnel and less political and strategic support from the global community. Additionally, the Iraqi forces were smaller and far less capable than they were in ODS. The first war plus twelve years of no-fly zone enforcement and sanctions weakened the Iraqi military considerably from its former self. OIF also had different strategic aims from ODS. ODS involved a limited objective to eject Iraqi forces and restore Kuwait's sovereignty, while OIF sought complete military victory and regime change. Coalition planners also incorporated many of the lessons learned from the first Gulf War into plans for the second effort.

---

[80]Ibid., 316.

OIF also demonstrated a much different operational approach from ODS. Unlike ODS's largely separate, sequenced air and ground operations, OIF actually began with a ground invasion the day before air operations started. General Tommy Franks, the coalition commander, desired to quickly seize Iraq's southern oil fields before they could be set ablaze. He also wanted to seize Tallil Air Base near An Nasiriyah intact for future logistics and aviation uses. Coalition planners believed the best way to accomplish these objectives was with a high tempo ground assault to kick off the campaign.

Leaders and planners emphasized speed to achieve these initial objectives and then capture Iraq's weapons of mass destruction before they could be used against coalition forces. The emphasis on speed necessitated seizure and control, rather than destruction, of many key pieces of Iraqi infrastructure, most notably the bridges along the avenue of approach to Baghdad. With these constraints in mind, coalition planners relied more heavily on heavy ground power from the beginning of OIF than they did in ODS. These measures enabled coalition forces to reach Baghdad in the famous "Thunder Run" on 7 April 2003; just over two weeks after operations began.

Cutting-edge technologies from ODS were mature and well integrated by the start of OIF. The once novel global positioning system (GPS) devices from ODS were tremendously refined by OIF and were used by practically all of the coalition forces. Additionally, GPS technology added an all-weather precision-guided weapon to the air component's arsenal with Joint Direct Attack Munitions (JDAMs). JDAMs paid especially large dividends for coalition forces during the infamous sandstorm between 24 and 27 March 2003. The storm that would have ceased air attacks during ODS merely slowed them down during OIF. During OIF, Joint Surveillance Targeting and Reconnaissance Systems (JSTARS) aircraft detected enemy movements despite the weather, and coalition fighters dropped precision-guided weapons through the storms without seeing their targets. The same storm was quite problematic for ground forces that bogged down with little to no visibility on the ground.

Once again, OIF featured stealth and PGM technology to execute precision strikes against leadership, and command and control assets from the beginning of the conflict. Air planners had over a decade since ODS to refine operational art featuring such technologies. The most notable attack came on the very first night of the war when two F-117 Nighthawk stealth fighters dropped 2000-pound JDAMs on a site where Saddam Hussein and his sons reportedly were meeting.[81] Although the bombs hit their mark, the intended targets were not killed, but the attack presumably achieved the psychological effect of putting Iraqi leadership on the defensive. It did not, however, cause the immediate and total collapse of the Iraqi system that was hoped for through the "shock and awe" campaign.

Ground forces also leveraged new technologies during OIF to a much greater extent then they did during ODS. M1A2 Abrams tanks had better targeting and protection systems compared to their earlier variants in ODS. Soldiers utilized night vision devices to a much wider extent in OIF than in ODS. Although there were no drastic technological revolutions between the wars, many of the preexisting devices were far more capable than they were during the first Iraq war. These improvements led to unprecedentedly low loss and casualty rates.

Both air and ground forces benefitted from refinements in unmanned aerial vehicles (UAVs).[82] The unmanned systems provided new levels of reconnaissance capabilities across the board, and they also demonstrated the ability to execute precision strikes on point targets. Examples of such strikes came when an Air Force Predator UAV fired a Hellfire missile to destroy an Iraqi ZSU-23-4 antiaircraft system on 22 March, and later when another Predator-shot

---

[81]Williamson Murray and Robert H. Scales, Jr., *The Iraq War* (Cambridge, MA: The Belknap Press of Harvard University, 2003), 155.

[82]UAVs are now called RPA, or remotely piloted aircraft, by the Air Force.

Hellfire destroyed a television antenna the Iraqis attempted to protect by placing it next to the Grand Mosque in Baghdad.[83]

Despite its success, the speedy ground advance toward Bagdad also highlighted some problems concerning supply consumption rates in the heavy units. Coalition planners estimated daily fuel consumption close to two million gallons per day through the first two weeks of the war, and then higher fuel consumption rates after that.[84] Planners mitigated the fuel issue through years of detailed planning and preparation, but had problems elsewhere. Despite careful planning, logisticians still had difficulty supplying ammunition, food, water, and maintenance supplies around 30 March.[85] The supply shortage forced the coalition to pause prior to assaulting Baghdad, disrupting the desired operational tempo.

Assessment

Twelve years of technological improvements widened the capability gap between coalition forces and the Iraqi military during OIF. The same devices that were in their infancies during ODS had become well-refined instruments in the years between the wars. There were numerous technology demonstrations throughout the war, from GPS-guided weapons striking point targets through the sandstorm, to remotely piloted systems executing precision strikes against sensitive or emerging targets, to armor and targeting systems that improved tank protection and lethality. The end result was a joint force that was far more capable than it was during the first Gulf War, a decade earlier.

Battle damage assessment remained problematic during OIF, despite considerable advancements in reconnaissance technologies. The decapitation effort on 20 March 2003 is a

---

[83]Walter J. Boyne, *Operation Iraqi Freedom* (New York: Tom Doherty Associates, 2003), 71.

[84]Gregory Fontenot, E. J. Degen, and David Tohn, *On Point; US Army in Operation Iraqi Freedom* (Fort Leavenworth, KS: Combat Studies Institute Press, 2004), 146.

[85]Boyne. *Operation Iraqi Freedom*, 124.

perfect example. Despite perfect hits on target, coalition planners could not determine whether or not Saddam Hussein and his inner circle were killed in the attack. After the war the same battle damage contentions emerged as those that typified ODS, with both air and ground forces seeking credit for vehicle kills on the battlefield. The high tempo operation combined with a three-day sandstorm made it difficult to determine who killed what in the race to Baghdad.

The most important takeaway is that coalition forces successfully advanced from Iraq's southern border to Baghdad and beyond, over 300 miles, in under three weeks. They managed this feat with minimal friendly losses, minimal civilian casualties, and very low collateral damage. The accomplishment was due to improved efficacy for both air and ground forces, along with the most integrated joint operations concept in war seen to date. No single actor or type of force was directly creditable for the victory. Coalition forces achieved victory with a combination of the factors outlined in the case study above.

Observations

The case studies of ODS and OIF proved one key point – airpower and ground power were both highly effective in their roles in both wars. Success in both wars is creditable to the wide technology gap that existed between the two sides. Coalition forces fought with cutting-edge American and European equipment while the Iraqis employed archaic Soviet systems that had long passed their prime. The measure/countermeasure dynamic discussed in Chapters 2 and 3 highly favored coalition forces. Effectiveness also increased between the wars with improvements to existing technology and with the introduction of UAVs, which benefitted both force components.

The studies also showed that it is difficult, if not impossible to declare one force component better than the other for use in war. Fog, friction, and personal bias during war skew data too much for it to be considered completely reliable. This problem will remain relevant until reconnaissance technology can definitively and accurately assess battle damage. What is more, there are secondary and tertiary effects in war that cannot be measured by any quantitative measure. Nighttime stealth precision attacks, or massed armor formations carry tremendous psychological power that can only be measured qualitatively. Evidence of such qualitative effects came with the post-conflict research that discovered Iraqi tank crews were afraid to operate their tanks and surface-to-air missile systems for fear of being killed. While this psychological effect could not necessarily be counted, it certainly had a massive impact on outcomes of the wars.

Investigating the two wars showed that airpower and heavy ground power both filled their respective roles, but those roles were very diverse. The diversity was more noticeable during ODS when coalition forces spent forty-three days preparing the battlefield for invasion solely through graduated air operations that began with strategic targets and worked downward toward operational and tactical-level targets. OIF was a much more joint operation from the outset of hostilities, but each force component specialized in missions that played to its personal strengths.

The case studies also highlight the importance of good operational planning that matches the right force component with the right conditions. Airpower is most effective and efficient when operating independent of ground forces, requiring minimal coordination and with little or no fratricide risk. Ground power is most effective and efficient when fighting in a prepared area of operations where the adversary's combat power is already reduced. The two force components produce mutually beneficial effects when their strengths are played off one another. For example, air interdiction to destroy adversary targets in a staging area weakens that force to enhance the ground effort when friendly forces make contact. Alternatively, ground forces can destroy adversary forces in close combat, encouraging reinforcement that exposes secondary forces to air interdiction. The operational artist must predict when and where those types of conditions exist to maneuver forces at the appropriate time and space. This concept links back to Fuller's principle of economy of force.

Chapter 7 – Conclusion

Armor and airpower both emerged during World War I as means to end the stalemate along the Western Front. Early theorists saw different ways that each type of machine should be used. Armor theorists intended their invention to break through enemy lines, creating a shallow penetration that could be exploited by cavalry and infantry. Airpower theorists, on the other hand, wanted their airplanes to bypass front line forces and strike right at the enemy's center of gravity, his capital city and vital interests. Both schools believed their weapons would end World War I and become the dominant weapon in future conflicts.

In roughly a full century of theory development, neither camp strayed far from its roots. Heavy ground forces are designed to excel in close combat situations, leveraging superior firepower and protection abilities. Air forces still aim for the adversary's strategic center of gravity first, and then work backward to support friendly ground forces. For airpower, the strategic approach changed somewhat over the years. Attacking enemy vital centers and civilian populations became inducing strategic paralysis by disrupting the enemy's ability to meaningfully observe his environment or direct his own forces toward his strategic aim.

Airpower and ground power are both quantum leaps ahead of their ancestors in terms of capabilities and effectiveness. Both are faster, can travel further, are better protected, and are far more precise and lethal with their weapons. Both forces, however, have been subject to measure/countermeasure races that offset their advances. These races mean that technological overmatches are generally small and short-lived for both airpower and ground power.

When comparing ground power to air power, it becomes quickly evident that the two forces possess very different qualities. These different qualities drive each force's capabilities, and "destruction of enemy forces" is the only overlapping capability between the two forces. The other capabilities link back to characteristics of each component that were built into its design at birth. Capabilities create missions and tasks that each component performs, and these missions and tasks are just as diverse as the characteristics from which they originate. These diverse tasks can be very complimentary when the two force components are jointly employed.

Effectiveness, efficiency, and efficacy, all revolve around economy of force. According to Fuller, economy of force simply means using your forces wisely to achieve the desired result without wasting effort. Efficacy is the measurement of how well those forces are used to achieve the desired result. It is a qualitative measurement, and therefore is difficult to measure with any scientific precision.

The two wars in Iraq showed that both heavy ground power and airpower were highly effective in combat operations while executing their doctrinal tasks and missions. Neither force was decisive in and of itself though. Airpower created the conditions for ground power to succeed by achieving and maintaining air superiority, and by creating confusion and disorder in the enemy system. Armor and heavy forces led ground efforts to close with the enemy and seize terrain. Heavy forces also flushed out enemy forces, thereby making them more vulnerable to air attack. Greater airpower effectiveness, in turn, enhanced ground power effectiveness. The symbiotic relationship between the two force components led to victory in both wars. Iraq is a unique case though, for the measure/countermeasure dynamic weighed heavily in favor of coalition forces. The technological gap in ODS was even wider by OIF.

The monograph deemed it impossible and unnecessary to compare efficacy between airpower and heavy ground power in the abstract, but rather to examine efficacy of each force component in context. Both force components contribute in very diverse ways to joint operations, and both are absolutely necessary in major combat operations. Rather than compare these two force components independently, researchers should study the effectiveness, efficiency, and efficacy of the combination of these two components. Operational artists must use their knowledge of airpower and heavy ground power to determine the times and places where each works best in specific circumstances. The synergistic effect of the two forces working together toward the same strategic aim produces results that neither component could achieve individually.

Bibliography

Books

Andrews, William F. *Airpower Against an Army: Challenge and Response in CENTAF's Duel with the Republican Guard.* Maxwell AFB, AL: Air University Press, 1998.

Borque, Stephen A. *Jayhawk! The VII Corps in the Persian Gulf War.* Washington, DC: Department of the Army, 2002.

Boyne, Walter J. *Operation Iraqi Freedom.* New York: Tom Doherty Associates, 2003.

Cameron, Robert S. *Mobility, Shock, and Firepower: The Emergence of the U.S. Army's Armor Branch, 1917-1945.* Washington, DC: United States Army Center of Military History, 2008.

Citino, Robert M. *Armored Forces; History and Sourcebook.* Westport, CT: Greenwood Press, 1994.

Clancy, Tom with General Chuck Horner. *Every Man a Tiger.* New York: Putnam Publishing Group, 1999.

Clausewitz, Carl Von. *On War.* Edited and translated by Michael Howard and Peter Paret. Princeton, NJ: Princeton University Press, 1976.

Cohen, Elliot A. *Gulf War Air Power Survey, Volume II: Operations and Effects and Effectiveness.* Washington, DC: United States Department of the Air Force, 1993.

Cohen, Elliot A., and Thomas A. Kearney. *Gulf War Air Power Survey, Summary Report.* Washington, DC: United States Department of the Air Force, 1993.

Crosby, Francis. *A Handbook of Fighter Aircraft.* London: Anness Publishing, 2002.

Deptula, David A. *Effects Based Operations: Change in the Nature of Warfare.* Arlington, VA: Aerospace Education Foundation, 2001.

Douhet, Giulio. *The Command of the Air.* Translated by Dino Ferrari. Washington, DC: Office of Air Force History, 1983.

Fontenot, Gregory, E. J. Degen, and David Tohn. *On Point; US Army in Operation Iraqi Freedom.* Fort Leavenworth, KS: Combat Studies Institute Press, 2004.

Fuller, J. F. C. *Armored Warfare.* Westport, CT: Greenwood Press, 1943.

———. *Foundations of Science and War.* Reprint, Fort Leavenworth, KS: U.S. Army Command and General Staff College Press, 1990. http://www.cgsc.edu/carl/resources/csi/fuller2/fuller2.asp#194 (accessed 19 August 2011).

———. *Machine Warfare.* Richmond, VA: Garrett and Massie, 1943.

Givens, Robert P. *Turning the Vertical Flank: Airpower as a Maneuver Force in the Theater Campaign.* Maxwell AFB, AL: Air University Press, 2002.

Green, William, and Gordon Swanborough. *The Complete Book of Fighters.* New York: Barnes and Noble Books, 1998.

Guderian, Heinz. *Achtung Panzer!* Translated by Christopher Duffy. London: Wellington House, 1992.

———. *Panzer Leader.* New York: Ballantine Books, 1957.

Hogg, Ian. *Tank Killing: Anti-Tank Warfare by Men and Machines.* New York: Sarpedon, 1996.

Houlahan, Thomas. *Gulf War: The Complete History.* New London, NH: Schrenker Military Publishing, 1999.

Lambeth, Benjamin S. *NATO's Air War for Kosovo: A Strategic and Operational Assessment.* Santa Monica, CA: RAND, 2001.

Leonhard, Robert R. *The Art of Maneuver: Maneuver Warfare Theory and AirLand Battle.* Presidio, CA: Ballantine Publishing Group, 1991.

Lind, William S. *Maneuver Warfare Handbook.* Boulder, CO: Westview Press, 1985.

Luttwak, Edward N. *Strategy: The Logic of War and Peace.* Cambridge, MA: Harvard University Press, 1987.

Mason, Tony. *Airpower: A Centennial Approach.* London: Brassey's, 1994.

Meilinger, Phillip S. *Airmen and Air Theory: A Review of the Sources.* Maxwell Air Force Base, AL: Air University Press, 2001.

———. *The Paths of Heaven: The Evolution of Airpower Theory.* Maxwell Air Force Base, AL: Air University Press, 1997.

Mitchell, William. *Winged Defense.* New York: Putnam's Sons, 1927.

Murray, Williamson, and Robert H. Scales, Jr. *The Iraq War.* Cambridge, MA: The Belknap Press of Harvard University, 2003.

Pirnie, Bruce R., Alan Vick, Adam Grissom, Karl P. Mueller, and David T. Orletsky. *Beyond Close Air Support; Forging a New Air-Ground Partnership.* Arlington, VA: RAND Corporation, 2005.

Stone, John. *The Tank Debate: Armour and the Anglo-American Military Tradition.* London: Harwood Academic Publishers, 2000.

Swinton, Ernest D. *Eyewitness.* London: Hodder and Stoughton, 1932.

Van Creveld, Martin, Steven L. Canby, and Kenneth S. Browner. *Air Power and Maneuver Warfare.* Maxwell AFB, AL: Air University Press, July 1994.

Warden, John A. III. *The Air Campaign: Planning for Combat.* Washington, DC: National Defense University Press, 1988.

Watts, Barry D. *The Foundations of US Air Doctrine: The Problem of Friction in War.* Maxwell Air Force Base, AL: Air University Press, 1984.

Wilbeck, Christopher W. *Sledgehammers; Strengths and Flaws of Tiger Tank Battalions in World War II.* Bedford, PA: The Aberjona Press, 2004.

Wright, Patrick. *Tank: The Progress of a Monstrous War Machine.* New York: Penguin Group, 2000.

Zucchino, David. *Thunder Run.* New York: Grove Press, 2004.

Government Documents

Belasco, Amy. *The Cost of Afghanistan, Iraq, and Other Global War on Terror Operations Since 9/11.* Washington, DC: Congressional Research Service, 2011.

Cone, Robert W. "Briefing on Joint Lessons Learned from Operation Iraqi Freedom." Media Presentation by director, Joint Center for Lessons Learned, U.S. Joint Forces Command, 2 October 2003.

Department of Defense. *Conduct of the Persian Gulf Conflict: Final Report to Congress.* Washington, DC: Government Printing Office, 1992.

———. Joint Publication 3-0, *Doctrine for Joint Operations.* Washington, DC: Government Printing Office, 2011.

———. Joint Publication 3-09, *Doctrine for Joint Fire Support.* Washington, DC: Government Printing Office, 2010.

———. Joint Publication 3-09.3, *JTTP for Close Air Support.* Washington, DC: Government Printing Office, 2009.

———. Joint Publication 3-33, *Joint Force Capabilities.* Washington, DC: Government Printing Office, 1999.

———. *Quadrennial Defense Review Report.* Washington, DC: Government Printing Office, 12 February 2011.

Department of the Army. "Army Battle Casualties and Non-Battle Deaths in World War II." Report, Washington, DC, 25 June 1953.

US Air Force. Air Force Doctrine Document (AFDD) 1, *Air Force Basic Doctrine.* Washington, DC: United States Department of the Air Force, 17 November 2003.

———. Air Force Doctrine Document (AFDD) 3-1, *Air Warfare.* Washington, DC: United States Department of the Air Force, 17 September 2010.

———. Air Force Doctrine Document (AFDD) 3-03, *Counterland Operations*. Washington, DC: United States Department of the Air Force, 17 September 2010.

———. "Air Force Performance in Desert Storm." White Paper, 1991.

US Army. Field Manual 3-0, *Operations*, Change 1. Washington, DC: United States Department of the Army, February 2011.

———. Field Manual 3-90, *Tactics*. Washington, DC: United States Department of the Army, July 2001.

———. Field Manual 3-90.5, *The Combined Arms Battalion*. Washington, DC: United States Department of the Army, 1 April 2008.

———. Field Manual 3-90.6, *The Brigade Combat Team*. Washington, DC: United States Department of the Army, 4 August 2006.

Theses/Monographs/Briefings

Boyd, John R. "Destruction and Creation." Essay, September 1976.

———. "Patterns of Conflict." Briefing, December 1986. http://www.ausairpower.net/ JRB/poc.pdf (accessed 11 August 2011).

Jacoby, Charles H. Jr. "In Search of a Quick Decision: The Myth of the Independent Air Campaign." Monograph, School of Advanced Military Studies, Fort Leavenworth, KS, 1991.

Kovich, Andrew S. "USAF Relevance in the 21st Century: A First Quarter Team in a Four Quarter Game." Research Paper, Air Command and Staff College, Air University, Maxwell AFB, AL, 2005.

Magee, Robert E. Lee. "Go Big or Go Home; Employing America's Heavy Force." Monograph, School of Advanced Military Studies, Fort Leavenworth, KS, 2010.

Russell, Steven D. "Picking the Right Horse? Dominant Maneuver in the Twenty-First Century." Thesis, U.S. Army Command and General Staff College, Fort Leavenworth, KS, 1998.

Journals

Flight Magazine. "A Girdle Round the Earth." 10 March 1949. http://www.flightglobal.com/ pdfarchive/view/1949/1949%20-%200461.html (accessed 16 May 2011).

Haun, Phil M. "Airpower versus a Fielded Army: A Construct for Air Operations in the Twenty-First Century." *Aerospace Power Journal* (Winter 2001). http://www.airpower.au.af.mil/ airchronicles/apj/apj01/win01/haun.html (accessed 20 March 2011).

Hinman, Ellwood P. IV. "Counterair and Counterland; Concepts for the 21st Century." *Joint Forces Quarterly* (First Quarter, 2008): 85-91.

Krepinevich, Andrew F. Jr. "The Army and Land Warfare: Transforming the Legions." *Joint Forces Quarterly* (Autumn 2002): 76-82.

Warden, John A. III. "Chapter 4: Air Theory for the 21st Century." *Air and Space Power Journal* (September 1995). http://www.airpower.maxwell.af.mil/airchronicles/battle/chp4.html (accessed 19 August 2011).

Internet/Other Sources

Boeing. History, "B-29 Superfortress." http://www.boeing.com/history/boeing/b29.html (accessed 16 May 2011).

Dictionary.com. "Effective." http://dictionary.reference.com/browse/effective (accessed 20 March 2011).

Dictonary.com. "Efficient." http://dictionary.reference.com/browse/efficient (accessed 20 March 2011).

Gates, Robert M. "United States Military Academy at West Point." 25 February 2011. http://www.defense.gov/speeches/speech.aspx?speechid=1539 (accessed 20 March 2011).

Keyes, Charley. "Defense secretary announces billions in budget cuts." *CNN.com*. 6 January 2011. http://articles.cnn.com/2011-01-06/politics/pentagon.budget.cuts_1_defense-budget-gates-plan-defense-secretary-robert-gates?_s=PM:POLITICS (accessed 20 March 2011).

Miles, Donna. "Carter: Budget Cuts Demand More DoD Buying Power." *American Forces Press Service*, 20 April 2011. http://www.defense.gov/news/newsarticle.aspx?id=63633 (accessed 20 March 2011).

www.ingramcontent.com/pod-product-compliance
Lightning Source LLC
Chambersburg PA
CBHW080554290526
45790CB00006B/2649